Somewhere Near Defiance

ANHINGA PRESS

Other books by Jeff Gundy

Poetry Collections
Spoken among the Trees (2007)
Deerflies (2004)
Rhapsody with Dark Matter (2000)
Flatlands (1995)
Inquiries (1992)

Poetry Chapbooks
Greatest Hits 1986-2003 (2003)
Surrendering to the Real Things (1986)
Johnny America Takes on Mother Nature (1975)

Essays/Creative Nonfiction
Songs from an Empty Cage: Poetry, Mystery, Anabaptism, and Peace (2013)
Walker in the Fog: On Mennonite Writing (2005)
Scattering Point: The World in a Mennonite Eye (2003)
A Community of Memory: My Days with George and Clara (1996)

SOMEWHERE NEAR DEFIANCE

POEMS

JEFF GUNDY

ANHINGA PRESS
TALLAHASSEE, FLORIDA 2014

Cover photograph: "A beautiful warm summer sunset at Weir's Rapids on the
    Maumee river in northwest Ohio." © Michael Shake / Shutterstock.com
Author photograph: Bill Walker
Cover and text design: Carol Lynne Knight
Type Styles: titles set in Lithos Pro and text set in Adobe Jensen Pro

Library of Congress Cataloging-in-Publication Data
Somewhere Near Defiance by Jeff Gundy, First Edition
ISBN – 978-1-934695-37-1
Library of Congress Cataloging Card Number – 2013952496

Anhinga Press Inc. is a nonprofit corporation
dedicated wholly to the publication and appreciation
of fine poetry and other literary genres.

For personal orders, catalogs
and information write to:
Anhinga Press
P.O. Box 3665
Tallahassee, Florida 32315
Website: www.anhinga.org
Email: info@anhinga.org

Published in the United States
by Anhinga Press
Tallahassee, Florida
First Edition, 2014

For Scott Russell Sanders,
who long ago taught me something
about living near Defiance.

Contents

Acknowledgments

Many thanks to the editors of the journals where these poems first appeared, some in different form:

About Place: "Kelley's Island Elegy with Wind and Innuendo"

Adirondack Review: "On the River of Doubt with TR and the Boys"

Arsenic Lobster: "The Passenger," "Contemplation with Borrowed Tent"

Atlanta Review: "Story Problem near Vancouver Island"

Basilica Review: "Contemplation with Distant Scenes and Loon"

Cape Rock: "Somewhere Near Defiance"

Center for Mennonite Writing Journal: "On the Birthday of Ronald Reagan and My Mother-in-Law, I Mourn Jerry Garcia," "Autobiography with *Blonde on Blonde*," "Interior Archeology"

Christian Century: "Evening Rhapsody between Madison and Whitewater," "Yellow Trail at Laurelville on Rapture Day"

Cincinnati Review: "Moons," "Rumination with Night Sky and Cotton," "March Ode"

Fifth Wednesday: "Meditation with Wallet, Eyeglasses, and Little Riley Creek"

Hamilton Stone Review: "The Foreigner Attempts to Master Nonfiction Narrative," "It Was Snowing, and Going to Snow," "Robinson Goes Around Again," "Additional Assertions on Souls," "Contemplation on Lake Insula"

Image: "Passage," "No Path"

Kenyon Review: "Having It All Four Ways"

Lake Effect: "Meditation with Assorted Pronouns and Personas," "Meditation on Copepods and Obscure Information"

Maverick Magazine: "Interior Housekeeping," "Contemplation with Weary Travelers," "Oh"

North American Review: "Slippers"

Perspectives: "And They Kept Silence and Told No One," "Table"

Phoebe: "Driftwood"

Poetry East: "Kansas St., North Newton, November 26," "Checking the Messages"

Poetry Salzburg Review: "On the Way to the Glacier," "No Boundaries," "Contemplation on Rules and Lines"

Rhubarb: "Afternoon Walk with Mosquitos and Commentary via Simone Weil and Mike Edmiston," "Notes from the Faculty Meeting"

Saint Katherine Review: "Meditation with Muddy Woods and Swinging Bridge," "The Unreliable Narrator Remembers the *Martyrs Mirror* Conference"

Shenandoah: "Cuyahoga Evening with Distance and Absence"

The Sun: "Contemplation on Rain and Religion," "Walk with Grand-Dog and Wallace Stevens"

Vineyards: "Slippery Intimations on the Flood Plain," "Contemplation on Rules and Lines"

Wind Word: "Contemplation with Rainy Birdsong"

A Ritual to Read to Each Other: Poems in Conversation with William Stafford: "Why Empathy Must Be Discouraged in Late Capitalist Societies"

"Something the Winter Wren Didn't Say" won the 2013 Slippery Elm poetry contest.

Many thanks, also, to organizers and organizations that allowed me to travel to beautiful places, hang out with wonderful people, and scribble in my notebook: Kathy Landis and Wilderness Wind for a canoe trip on the Boundary Waters; Terry Hermsen, Otterbein University, and the Environmental Education Council of Ohio for ongoing workshops in Cuyahoga Valley National Park; Paul Merchant, Kim Stafford and Fred Marchant for a workshop at the William Stafford symposium in

Portland; Rudy and Irene Martens for a cruise up the Inside Passage; Dan and Karen Ruth for sharing their Michigan cottage; the Quarry Hollow writing group for years of support and stimulation; the William J. Fulbright Commission for a semester in Salzburg; Bluffton University for a sabbatical and for ongoing support.

For their presence, conversation, and advice poetic and otherwise, I am especially grateful to Kirsten Beachy, Susan Carpenter, Terry Hermsen (again), Jean Janzen, Julia Spicher Kasdorf, Julia Levine, Clint McCown, Phil Metres, Keith Ratzlaff, and Kevin Stein. Thanks to my bright and strapping sons Nathan, Ben, and Joel, my smart, tough, and lovely daughters-in-law Jessica Witmer and Jennifer Ruth, and (always) to Marlyce.

Somewhere Near Defiance

I.

SOMEWHERE NEAR DEFIANCE

It's late but everything comes next.
  — Naomi Shihab Nye, "Jerusalem"

1.

I live near Defiance, a white name pressed on an old place.
Mad Anthony Wayne's soldiers broke down the orchards

when the battle was theirs, and built a fort
where the Auglaize and Maumee Rivers meet.

Water will answer anything: the moon, the wind,
the mud. The rivers mingle and move on.

2.

Once I drove my little car right into the heart of the empire,
huddled with my friends to plot and complain. All over town

the poets and other malcontents were hiding in the open,
vowing to split the rocks and terrify the despots.

In the coffeehouse we tallied our losses and wondered how
to subvert the lyric *I* until the hot waitress grabbed the mike

to say that racism wasn't over yet. We clapped for her,
then wandered toward the Capitol, launched some ragged

words to each other and the wind. All right, you can
have *shock*, we told the adversary, but *awe* belongs to us.

3.

Walt Whitman thought his poems might stop the war.
When they did not he moved to Washington, took a day job

so he could go to the field hospitals, read to the wounded,
write letters for men with no arms or eyes. *I have been hurt*

but am mending well. Do not weep, I will find you one day.
I walked around for days, found no field hospitals,

lots of monuments. I passed the suited and booted,
shaggy and lame, proud and weary, and it seemed

that each of us carried a wound we were trying to hide.

4.
Meanwhile the drone pilots turn their Hellfires loose
from dark rooms in the suburbs, buy a 6-pack on the way home.

1200 veterans of the last good war die each day,
and the stools at the VFW stand like puzzled mushrooms.

5.
These days I wake up grateful that my heavy dreams are gone.
I snag the zipper of my coat, pull it free, and walk off

puzzling over slides and words and stratagems. Then I step
into a room and see a row of faces, hopeful and new

as yellow apples hanging in the orchards of Defiance.

6.
The morning came brilliant to my quiet town,
sun in the junipers, a robin on the wire.

Nothing that I do matters to the earth or the sky.

But I've stalled around too long — it's time for declarations,
time for floods. Time to put down the *Toledo Blade*

and take a very long walk. Time to say peace on terror,
peace on drugs, peace on Defiance.

Peace on Mad Anthony and his soldiers — gone so quiet now —
and the warriors they fought, and the fruit trees they tore.

The Auglaize and the Maumee join and drift on,
exchanging sticks and soil and bits of news.

We are in the earth already, and the earth in us.

Even from Defiance, nothing's more than half a world away.

Meditation with Wallet, Eyeglasses, and Little Riley Creek

> *The weak force of God settles down below in the hidden interstices of*
> *being, insinuated into the obscure crevices …*
> — *John D. Caputo, The Weakness of God*

Which card is it that will open the steel door?

I know that one card will take me anywhere, or almost, and another will tell
the authorities they should let me on the plane.

The Kingdom of God, says Caputo, is like a beautiful old poem whose
author is completely unknown.

My glasses have tiny rainbow sparkles on each lens, spreading as I scrape at
them. The anti-scratch coating is separating, the office worker says sweetly,
sometimes that happens, sorry they are not under warranty, well it's been
two years and I will have to ask the doctor, what if something has changed?

The idea of one true religion, Caputo says, makes no more sense than the
idea of one true poem.

For the fourth day in a row the brown roar of the creek bears tons of topsoil
and effluvia toward the ocean.

Is there one true creek?

God is a *weak* force, says Caputo, a call, an event, a voice. All the rest is
rouged and painted theology, the invention of men wishing to be strong.

If I scrape the anti-scratch coating entirely away, will I see something new?

If God is great but not strong … I take a deep breath, let it out.

A wren in the pine tree, pecking at the new cones, visible only when it moves.

It leaves a branch quaking as it disappears.

THE FOREIGNER ATTEMPTS
TO MASTER NONFICTION NARRATIVE

When the soul gets tapped it gushes forth — but is the tapped soul
like a thawed waterfall? Like the grain behind the false wall

in *The Long Winter*, grimmest of the Little House books?
Here are the lopsided fruits of grief: a wooden shower stall

and a three-toed sloth. What lie is more self-indulgent
than a sentence beginning "To be very honest"? And facts,

facts just muddy up the story, which is yours after all.
Say "I imagined," and you can say any damn thing.

Comparison is fundamental and useless. One must ferry
readers toward the epiphany, then dump them out of the boat.

I had a free house, though I hated it, and access to a messy
but massive archive. The minotaur did not reveal himself.

All this I, I, I may seem myopic, but these fine, paranoiac particles
persist, as does my yearning for salt, grease, stray factoids,

and the words written on back of the scratch paper.
White canes can be mailed free. Scorpions must be sent

by surface mail. Bearded dragons may be freely transported
through Detroit, but print and sign the form for the convenience

of the border guards. The novel began in the city, with the problem
of life in such close quarters. I am trying now to be grateful

for wretched excess, for the abundance of blizzards. I have
good folders labeled Doubt and Belief, but items keep shifting

between them, or into the third folder, which will hold no label.
So much that once glowed seems dull today; still, a window

of free water glints below the bridge. When seeking the portage,
I learned, the secret is to find the place where the water moves.

Autobiography with "Blonde on Blonde"

The ragman drew circles on everything, but St. John dragged
his feet through them all, saying, *In the beginning was the Word!*

until time shuddered like a bus with bad brakes and my dad
rubbed his face and sat down at the kitchen table, his farmer tan

glowing. It had been a windy day, and the brutal stench
of Hillman's hogs wafted through the screens. I whacked Kathy

on the back of the head just to hear her howl. It worked.
Then they drove me off to college, where I learned

that the not-yet has already happened, if you squint at it
just right. *I am, I said*, said Neil Diamond, and we had

to agree with that. Then the president explained that those
unwilling to kill for peace might once have been good people,

but godless communist drugs had made them into trolls
and orcs. We knew he was an idiot — we were elves and hobbits —

and decided to set off for Mordor to destroy the Ring
right after dinner. But somebody put on *Blonde on Blonde* again,

and it was just like the night to play tricks, and we could hardly
root out the fascist pigs while Louise and her lover were so entwined.

We walked down beside the dam instead, tried to lose ourselves
in the scant woods. I never got to Memphis or to Mobile.

The hard rain was already falling, but the sun still shone like glory
some of those afternoons, with classes over and the long night ahead

and water roaring down the spillway like the great I AM.

It Was Snowing, and Going to Snow

Why was that girl at the door of the office, shy and shining?
I've got too many symptoms already, too many reasons

to stay home all night cruising the dumb cable, getting plump
on crackers and cheese. Who needs more drama?

Thousands of deer die every year right here in the heartland
and still they wander like heretics yearning for martyrdom.

It's just late, all my teams defeated, the lights dim and snow
threatening like the mafia all over town. I don't deserve anything

but I want two more chances, and a long holiday in Salzburg
or the south of France. If we can't protect the innocent,

how about the guilty? If you asked I might accept the tag,
dive into the ring and take your place with the grinning bruiser,

get stomped into painful pacifist righteousness. Consider
the signs and predictions, the soft and flirty forecasts

and the girl at the office door, hesitant, wanting to know
what I think. I think there's a nice little room for her

somewhere in my right brain, a bit close sometimes but warm
and snug and an easy walk downtown after the snow.

Forget hope and wish. See how the useless, lovely gift
scrunches and flattens under her tall leather boots.

ROBINSON GOES AROUND AGAIN

[E. A. Robinson] wrote Amy Lowell that at the age of six he sat in a
rocking chair and wondered why he had been born.
— Norton Anthology of Modern Poetry

He leaned out the window, feeling like his skin
was inside out. Get a room somebody yelled

but though he craned and peered he couldn't see
who was doing what. He exhaled and went back

to the rocking chair, moved some damp underwear.
The dryer belt had snapped again, it was four flights

down to the laundromat, and the whole place
was damp as the cracked tiles behind the toilet.

Maggie would be off work at five, hungry and tired.
The thought of cooking gave him a small, precise pain

between and just below his ears. He punched the remote
and watched two paunchy former stars insult a quarterback

while the same four bad clips played over and over.
At last they cut to commercial and he could let it go,

follow the fine web of cracking plaster up the wall,
across the ceiling, like a map of his interior and its roads:

crooked, in need of repair, and trailing off aimlessly
in all directions. The rocking chair didn't squeak much,

and it held him up. There was spaghetti, a can of sauce,
lettuce in a bag. Could he toast Maggie's jeans in the oven,

dance the room waving her wispy panties dry?
Was this the night she wouldn't come home at all?

WHY EMPATHY MUST BE DISCOURAGED
IN LATE CAPITALIST SOCIETIES

According to the latest studies, it all has to do with the mirror neurons,
the ones we can't afford to trust. Look at that face, try not to smile.

Next thing you know we'll be using the word *comrade*, or wrestling
happily in the mud, or forgetting our lost freedom to throw

the black folks out of town at sunset. For instance, there are cities
in Cuba not named Havana. The island is 1000 miles long,

but only 75 meters wide. Extremity in the pursuit of money is no vice,
but buying insulin for the 101-year old woman who's been part

of the domino game on her front porch since 1956 is aid and comfort.
You know. Just look in those eyes and say *godless enemy of freedom.*

You see how dangerous this is. Next thing you know we'll be
taking pictures and talking in whatever language these people speak,

demented or placid, high rise or low. We'll eat all the *arroz con pollo*
we're offered, smuggle in diapers if we can, find a place

in something bigger, or smaller, than we thought we deserved.
Indignation without action is froth, said Gladstone in 1896.

Mix those dominoes, listen to them click and spatter,
take seven. Who's got the double blank? Play it in the center.

First Notes on Border Crossings

Early images: distant horses, a loud Ethiopian restaurant
with backless stools, my enemy seated behind me at the next table,

demanding to be ignored. Tales of giant salamanders
hidden behind moist glass walls, of words abandoned in flame.

I grew up far from any border. I have more privilege than power.
The DMZ between the Koreas has become a lush natural landscape,

250 klicks long and 14 inches wide. Windsor, says the guy
from Detroit, is America Lite. I have been there, but never

to Mexico, much less for a six-week motorcycle tour. Truly
crossing any border means embracing error, at least your own.

Without anxiety, no one learns a language or another place.
What if the language of home is foreign to you? Could I spend

the next three days in silence, like a Quaker or a potted plant?
I want to be known without the trouble of knowing. No one else

can say who anyone is, or where you are from. We're always
talking back to Saussure: chanting, praying, casting spells,

in the labyrinthine lobby or on the dirt floor where the stone
rolls beneath me like a trick. In Polish *death* and *laughter* rhyme,

and the poem disintegrates as death does its business.
Rhyme makes a marriage, or at least a long secret affair

that makes us rethink everything. The poet of the wetlands imagines himself as a slug, as moss on the wall.

It is our nature to make a paradise of the other shore.

Rumination with Night Sky and Cotton

What you can't see may not matter. What you can barely see, those
dim stars and hints of nebulae, could mean no more than a tidal pool

drying out a week sooner or later, a menu with three entrees taped over,
the spindly trees balancing up and out of the old quarry's gravel.

How do you count the ways? How do you reckon arsenic and
adobe, Egyptian cotton and the fruit of the month arriving pithy

and soft in its cardboard cocoon, food even the pigs would scorn?
Our matches can be struck only on the box. Our colors are multiple,

pure, and inconsolable. Some stretches of highway are too crowded
and too lonesome for any vehicle made in this solar system.

Night after night all that music pours down from the stars
and disappears, night after night we roll the doors shut and fasten

both the locks, and the picnic table and the deck chairs hum
and quiver, quiver and hum, and the satellites shift and blink,

and the planes bent on Newark, Pittsburgh, Seoul roar through
somewhere in between, calculating everything, spinning hard,

burning what they must and scattering what's left behind them
like a trail of bread crumbs, or long-fiber cotton, or broken clouds.

INTERIOR HOUSEKEEPING

The burning city of my sorrow …
— *William Stafford*

My sorrow is not a city, and not burning. It is Railroad Street
in my town, so small it has only six houses, all facing

the tracks, three of them neat and clean, two in need
of paint and shingles, one so poor that nobody remembers

how to open the door, how long ago the gas was turned off,
what dwells and swells inside the dark refrigerator.

Maybe there's an old man in the bedroom upstairs,
drinking from the rusty sink tap, eating stale corn chips

and Oreos. His wife left a note, but it fell behind the stove.
He took what he could find upstairs a week ago, knowing

this was his last trip. He pared mold off the last wedge
of cheese with a table knife, then tried it on his arm.

Twice he heard the phone ring, the second time for an hour.
He remembered to put the cat outside. He ripped the bag

of food right down, filled the water dish. He locked the doors.
The sheets have flowers on them. The blanket is wool.

A family of squirrels is living in the wall near the chimney.
They scratch and chitter all night. He scratches back.

No Path

for Gordon Kaufman

Kayak on the quarry: will you hug the shore, push straight across,
waver or dawdle? No paths on the water. Almost November,

and the poison ivy is still green. The soft trap of sky closes
all around. An artful little spray of leaves near the shore,

as though Martha Stewart were sitting in for God.
Give up all that Father stuff, said Gordon, *look where it's got us.*

And the Warrior — even worse. The kayakers lift and dip
their paddles, orange signals: this way for us. So much is offered,

so much goes begging, and still what we need evades us, or hides
in plain sight. On the water, every way might be the right way.

God might be the Father and the Warrior and the lost leaves,
the water and the bleached trunk, motion and stone,

lush twists of cloud and barking dog and wind,
star upon star alert and invisible in every direction,

low moan in the blood, circle and drift in the bright cells,
shadowy hum and whir of electrons, fizz and buzz and shush

too small to name. No end, no opening, no tribe, no answer.
Only this: kayak and paddlers, lift and dip,

breath and muscle above the chill water, below the soft sky.

II.

HAVING IT ALL FOUR WAYS

By a primal oneness the four — earth and sky, divinities and mortals — belong together in one.
— Heidegger, "Building Dwelling Thinking"

Now I a fourfold vision see …
— Blake

Prologue

Triangles are very strong, but groups of three are unstable.

As for two, when is that enough except in bed? Even in bed?

And one, oh, we can never be alone in this world, the universe bends and we twist, it shudders and we shake, the clouds of witnesses bloom like gnats along the springtime trails.

So why use so much ink, grumpy, unsatisfied? Here are the graceful and portentous branches, the dependable water, the ether and the stone.

When will we find purchase in this world, if not in the grace and balance of the eternal four?

Some Inexact Examples of the Four Elements

Sweat, chocolate, lust, and fire.

Wheat straw, columbine, saffron, and the magic mountain.

William Blake, Patty Griffin, John Coltrane, and Colombian Supremo French Roast.

Straw for the garden, a hoe worn thin by sharpening, the first radishes, and one of those old Oliver tractors with a narrow front end.

An old oak desk with new varnish, a corkscrew willow, the wind circling the room like a curious spirit, and the voice calling, *Hey hon? You wanna start the grill?*

Now, whenever, should have, and maybe.

Catechism and Confession (Partial)

What have you read?
> *Too much, not enough.*

What have you seen?
> *Not enough, too much.*

What do you know?

Which of the sirens do you love?
> *The noon siren, for it means we all are safe.*

Which of the sirens do you love?
> *The late night siren, for it means I am safe.*

Which of the four stones do you love?
> *The black granite, or the red. No, the limestone.*
> *No, the stone I cannot name.*
> *No.*

Which do you love, mother or child?
> *The mother, because she does not look at me,*
> *because she has forgotten she is beautiful,*
> *because she is wearing her spring shorts,*
> *because she cares only for the child.*

Further Remarks

When the four elements have their mojo on, the fields tremble to be plowed

When the four elements are as instruments well in tune, the skies turn red though the sun is long gone

Where the four elements mingle in due proportion, there the old men startle upright in their limousines, tear up the secret agreements, disappear alone into the mountains

When the four elements speak in harmonious accord the boys and girls loiter around the swimming pool and saunter home the long way, towels hanging loose about their loins

When the four elements are truly named the spheres will lock and fuse and deliver us, the valleys be exalted and the rough places plain, the lion caress the lamb, the little streams of alcohol come trickling down the rocks

Where the number is four desire and beauty are two sides of the fourfold coin, inscribed along its edge and in its arc and spin, glinting on every surface, and in the watcher and the one who tosses, and the coin falls through the quivering air to the shimmering stone

When the number is four the naming will begin, names for the none, the many, the lost hidden squandered obliterated, the annihilated ridiculed scraped into plastic and dumped in the landfill, yes the names are difficult

Where number is four the great eye and its circles the ear and the voice sway and tremble into speech into silence into music into flesh

MEDITATION WITH MUDDY WOODS
AND SWINGING BRIDGE

> *[The covenant] is structured in violence and steeped in blood,*
> *from the blood of circumcision and endless animal slaughter to*
> *brutal extermination of the 'people of the land.'*
> — *Grace Jantzen, Violence to Eternity*

Hot wind from the west. Trail still soft after a whole week's drying.

Deer tracks, coon, one stubborn mud-hiker's deep scours, each like a little boat or a long wet nest.

Wood piled everywhere — neat rows for woodstoves, heaps of trash and branches.

We were in Salzburg when a great storm scattered the old trees on the Kapuzinerberg like pickup sticks.

Today I brought nothing but pens, keys, comb, notebook, bicycle, lock, wallet and credit cards.

And knees a big black fly seems to like, and shorts with a pocket ripped two summers ago, still not fixed.

Morning reading: What kind of God would drown every living thing that wouldn't fit on some puny ark? Would slaughter the people of Canaan for the sake of one hungry band of nomads?

Many good gravel paths lead from the subdivision into the woods, but only the animals use them.

Somebody's cutting something hard in a dry swimming pool.

Who discovered we could cast our anger at the sky and get it back named God?

In my old house the bathroom sink plugs up every four months but I know exactly how to swear and clear it.

Small white blooms all over the multiflora rose, bushes twice my size.

Seed pods float in the pond like mothers determined to tan whether or not their children get lost in the bushes.

On a day this hot and green it seems crazy to think that God picks sides.

One plank of the swinging bridge is missing, one bowed and soft, and a big lost branch is wedged high between the end posts, but I walk across it anyway.

SLIPPERS

I used to believe I could be a crow, or a pheasant running
long-tailed and pretty down the rows of broken stalks,

oblivious of shotguns. I used to believe in spontaneous rebirth,
in the multiplicity of rewards, in the indefinite renewal

of overdue books. I used to dream of the wearying privilege
of travel, the miraculous beauty tapping at the motel door

at 2 a.m., saying, *It's Angel.* I used to believe that each step
was easy, and that I could recover from any fall. I used to run

and never get tired in the humid summer dusk, playing horses
with my cousins at somebody's birthday party, through

the ditch lilies and the high grass. I did not believe then
that every step contained a fall. I had never watched a man

work his way slowly from wheelchair to car seat, his shirt
and pale belly spilling out. I would never have thought

the snow would pile this deep, would last this long, that I would
walk the icy narrow paths looking down, leaning forward,

careful as any man who has fallen more than once,
any man thinking of his Christmas slippers and soft chair

just a hundred steps away, a dozen. I used to believe
that every step was too slow, that I would run faster next year,

that I would rise up stronger each time I fell, spitting out
the mouthpiece, my whole body singing from the stranger's

helmet, from the stranger's body breaking over mine.

THE REPENTANT ANABAPTIST RESPONDS BELATEDLY TO THE READER'S REPORT

> *The Fathers … do not sit at their desks like the Scholastics in order to do theology, because when the Church Fathers theologize, speculation or reflection is strictly forbidden … If and when someone reaches theosis, he will know from the very experience of theosis precisely what is meant by the sayings and concepts that he comes across in the Bible … [the Fathers] wrote what they wrote on the basis of this experience and because of this experience what they wrote is divinely inspired.*
> — Father John Romanides, *Patristic Theology*, 85-86.

Thank you for your authoritative critique. I have heard the Word and seek to obey.

I have sought earnestly not to allow your criticism to come across as unintentional praise.

I accept that until and unless I myself enter theosis, repentance and obedience are the only appropriate responses.

I desire to be shaped into a deeply grateful and holy being.

I will learn both Greek and Russian to peruse the sacred wisdom of the Fathers.

I see now even in translation that the path to true holiness is taking food only once a day on the second, fourth and sixth day of the week, eating about six ounces of bread, of dry food not to satiation, and drinking three or four cups of water.

I see now that when my people walked singing to the flames for believers, baptism and in refusal of the sword they were arrogant, delusional and possibly psychotic.

I accept the good Father's calm explanation of why the One who made the suns and worlds and creatures speaks only to the Fathers.

Had I understood this sooner my life might have been different.

Where I grew up diversity meant that my little town had Catholics and Mennonites as well as Lutherans and Methodists.

The last authority figure I trusted was my high school superintendent, who was six foot ten and after graduation told me, "There's always room at the top."

He turned out to have embezzled funds from the district for twenty years.

He didn't even apologize when he finally got busted.

Blame it on him.

No, blame it on me.

I should have listened to my teachers, especially the stupid ones, who tried to cure me.

I should have spent more time with the Fathers, though in my area they're even more thinly spread than Mennonites.

Instead of throwing that drunken soldier out of his garden Blake should have bowed and waited for instructions.

Dickinson should have given up her scribbling and earnestly sought the true way, though surrounded by all those Puritans she was shit out of luck anyway.

And we won't even start on that scoundrel Whitman.

Yes, my mother told me I needed to grow up when I slammed the closet door on my sister and almost cut off the tip of her little finger.

Yes I should have left for the desert the very next day, though the doctor got it sewed back on and my sister seems to have forgiven me.

Ask my children, my students, my wife: I've been patently silly and juvenile all my born days.

Ask my father-in-law, who winced every time we discussed my auto, family, life, property, and hail insurance until he got Alzheimer's and lost the ability to worry on my behalf.

I still owe money on the mortgage.

My lawn is a disgraceful muddle of dandelions and violets.

Still, I thank you. Now I contemplate William Blake and John Keats exchanging gorgeous and ineffectual screams as the flames cleanse them, and sweet Emily roasting in her willful pride and doubt,

Sharing her burning deck with Menno and Grebel and Marpeck and the dismal mother and heretic Anneken Jans, late of Rotterdam,

Who must herself have gone straight from flaming pyre to flaming pyre for her dread refusal to accept the Way of the Fathers forever and amen.

MEDITATION ON COPEPODS
AND OBSCURE INFORMATION

Some days I look around wildly,
convinced I'm missing something crucial.

Some days I pick up the guitar and try
to play toward something that won't fit

into words but might change the silence
where words grow, that place like

the liquid spaces within the living rock
in the salt-water tank where tiny

obscure creatures wait to be born.
You must look very closely to see

the copepods, smaller than rice grains,
translucent as rice fried in oil.

But once you know, you can watch them
crawl over the rock and each other,

feast on the purple and green algae,
delirious with delight, knowing

nothing of words or chords
or trains, the humming pumps

that make their weather,
the glass walls that keep them alive.

On the Birthday of Ronald Reagan and My Mother-in-Law, I Mourn Jerry Garcia

Water loose, raw and smelly all over town again, nearly as much as the last big flood, then it turned sharp and snowed a little and I frittered away the day finding clips from YouTube to reinforce my bitter lectures on the Cold War.

I walked home, switched computers, browsed and brooded some more, found Jerry Garcia plump and old in cut-off shorts, singing a heartbreaking "Peggy-O."

For a moment I rested in the old dream that sad lovely songs on the folly of war will make us stop killing each other.

Will you marry me, pretty Peggy-O? If you will marry me, I'll set your cities free … Jerry's gray hair blows in the wind. He looks nearly dead, and he is.

Reagan insisted that once the Russians knuckled under and found Jesus we could all be pals.

My mother-in-law, still living in blurry and complicated comfort in a condo in Surrey, BC, resembles him in ways that shall not be detailed here.

The snow stopped, and the streets began to freeze.

If ever I return, pretty Peggy-O … If ever I return, your cities I must burn, and destroy all the ladies in the aree-o.

Reagan led the so-called free world well after his dementia had begun to show. The Dead played thousands of shows. Jerry did not live a pure life.

After the somber, shimmery guitar solo, one more verse: *Sweet William, he is dead … and buried in the Lousiana country-o.*

And then our neighbors' blind basset hound Herald stepped out, and proclaimed the need for attention to small things moving in the soggy chilly night.

"And They Kept Silence and Told No One"

— Luke 9:36

Here we are tipping between Epiphany and Lent, the warm glow
and the ash. The garments of Jesus shine on the mountaintop,
Moses and Ezekiel mutter gravely in his ears, the disciples
are dazed and dazzled. If the question is what to give up, I have
some ideas: coffee, chocolate, and wanton thoughts are off the table,
but how about cocaine, hookers, tattoo parlors and *American Idol?*
Anyway what choice do we have, what we keep or lose?
The chilled robins wobble bravely above the grand, snowy wastes.
Even the wild cats, their best paths buried, are reduced to driveways
and sidewalks. But never mind. I'll throw in almost all my petty heresies
and my right to brood on every intransigent mystery except
why we're here at all. *I always look for Jesus in the eyes of other people,*
said the woman. You think I'm too jaded for that? I could give up
doubt, sarcasm, and passive aggression in a minute, and the simple
mean question too. Give up the balcony and sit in the middle pew.
Give up all my ends for golden means. Give up all means and
meander into Lent so moist and easy that the world will find
me worthy, open its long folds and welcome me in at last.

MEDITATION WITH ASSORTED PRONOUNS
AND PERSONAS

I still had two friends, but they were trees.
— Larry Levis

Here a small horde of mayflies under a damp ledge
as though nursing at the stone. Here a cave deep enough

for an hour's shelter from the rain. Here two near-lovers,
arm in arm, talking happily. And a few hundred hemlocks

and a million tons of stone, give or take, and quartz
pebbles working out from the sandstone

as the moss works its way down. Try to remember:
once you were so firm, so embedded, single-minded.

This stone like a ship's prow forcing a path
through the cool earth. You can't dig a hole

in water. You can't organize the air. You can cross
the road to either side and not find a chicken.

Take forever, take your time, take mine. Take
something hard and make it smooth. What if you could

crawl the world like an ant, belly and feelers close
to the greeny moss, the flaky stone? What if

your two best friends were a hemlock and a tulip poplar,
one casting an ancient spray of needles

and the other spindly and doomed to be shaded out
next summer? If I were you I'd holler, surely,

I'm so used to being me. If I tell you to and you rub
the back of your hand on the stinging nettle, just to try

it out, whose problem will it be if you break out
all over? If I put the book down on the gray stone,

if I fold out a page and rub it from above until the trace
of quartz and sandstone, moss and ants, is laid black

and shifty into the paper, whose marks will those be?

TABLE

The pen in my hand writes red, not quite blood. If I have a soul,
it might be like this, thin, wet, smelling of copper and iron.

Down on Riley Street, the Baptist workers have drained, cleaned,
and sanitized every flooded basement. They accepted no money

and didn't preach to anyone, knowing that every touch
leaves a trace anyway. If every slide along the banisters of lust

and gravity is both transient and irrevocable, in the next life
I could be a partisan or the brisk woman who runs the B & B.

I could be the psychic who uses the place to meet clients
who must not know where she lives. She sits with them

at the big table, calm as a forest pool, reading the weary pulses
of souls who rest their hands in hers. She feels, from another time,

the doctor whose ego is big as Montana — he sits at his high desk,
diplomas and portraits arrayed behind him like seals

from the almighty. He glowers, clears his throat, not unkindly.
He instructs a meek woman on the proper care of wounds.

And all the while he dreams he is a black dog padding through
luminous leaves, eyes nearly shut, sniffing out the warm prey.

THE UNRELIABLE NARRATOR REMEMBERS
THE MARTYRS MIRROR CONFERENCE

I. Preliminary Remarks

The full title: *The Bloody Theater or Martyrs Mirror of the Defenseless*
Christians Who Baptised Only Upon Confession of Faith,
and Who Suffered and Died for the Testimony of Jesus,
Their Saviour, From the Time of Christ to the Year A. D. 1660,
makes everything plain, if not simple.

In 1660 the author and Dutch churchman Thieleman J. Van Braght
was asked to answer for the boldness of his stance. He had stood firm
against the Collegiants, who baptized durn near anybody and
let sinners take communion, who said the True Church was
not only invisible but nowhere existed upon this earth.

His vast book asserted that the True Church remains
"visible, discernible, and distinguished from other nations,"
that a golden thread runs from the Lord Jesus Christ
through the defenseless martyrs of all ages, tormented,
burned, pressed hard by the many false Christians.
The errors, sins, and horrors of "the ungodly and false church"
are documented in fifteen large pages, under headings like
"Two, Three, and Four Popes Reigning at the Same Time."

These are sad and dangerous times, Van Braght said,
when Satan comes among the quiet and comfortable
in the twilight, in a strange yet pleasing form,
when the world reveals itself very beautiful and glorious,
pleasing to the lust of the flesh and the eye.
Mighty buildings, garments from abroad,
great dinners with no thought for the poor.

It sometimes seems to us, he said, *as if heaven had come
down upon earth, or that we were ascending from earth
to heaven. … We walk no longer upon earth with
our thoughts; nevertheless, we are still encompassed
by a cloud of earth, a body of clay, a heavy load of the soul.*

II. Miscellaneous Facts and Assertions

To make Van Braght's list, a martyr need only have been defenseless, a
believer in adult baptism, and of course a Christian.

The Ephrata *Martyrs Mirror* of 1748 was the largest printing project of
colonial America.

A million large sheets of paper were handmade and printed.

Leftover pages were confiscated for musket wadding in the Revolution,
and so the book became a body, torn and shredded, burned in its turn.

The recent English edition, with its grocery-sack cover and red-splattered
end pages, is far too large to read in bed.

When the body is burned its ash becomes words, its freed atoms
become story.

In the Catholic martyrology, innocent priests are murdered by hideous
mobs, the cathedrals desecrated, the holy relics smashed and plundered.

If the stories of wounds do not ring true for you, perhaps you have not
been sufficiently wounded.

A book needs to be touched, like a child or a silk sheet, like a handful of
raspberries, like a loaf of bread.

III. Questions for Discussion

Explain a) the relation between martyrdom and selflessness and b) the need for a crowd of onlookers.

How can one be sure that the Holy Spirit has guided the act of translation?

What language did Adam speak, and how might it be recovered?

"The self is nothing but a shifting concatenation of errors, flaws, and blunders." Discuss.

Compare and contrast: the martyr, the athlete, the gladiator.

If the book of a thousand stories has collapsed into the image of Dirk Willems turning back to pull his pursuer from the icy pond, what then?

What if the *Mirror* reflected something other, something more, than death?

What new, bright, stunning life might we glimpse among its myriad stories, its clouds of witnesses, its parade of fools and heroes, innocents and earnest explainers, its flames and blood?

What if we all are children left to hold a pear, or a twisted bit of metal, or the fading scent of the flesh that bore us into this world, caught for a moment more in our own fleeting bodies?

CHECKING THE MESSAGES

God is love,
they say,
in human words.
　　　　　— Franz Wright

One message reveals that the time is now.

Another includes a batch of complex activities
that somehow become "wins" and "losses."

I believe we must also consider
pink roses and stove pipe.

　　　Love is words
　　　God says
　　　in human.

One message is contained in all the ambitious brilliant novels
I have failed to read, well into my sixth decade.

Some nights the pattern on the rug
is all the information I can stand.

　　　They say, "Love
　　　God, human"
　　　in words.

One message I wrote on my hand in 1969 —
pages I was supposed to read for the next day
in a book full of lies, half-truths, and misdirections,
but also "Ozymandias" and "The Hollow Men."

Or did they say
the words
"Love human, God"?

One message is the kerosene lantern
we found in the garage when we moved in.
25 years later I still think I'll clean it up
and use it someday. I admire its patience
and calm, how slowly it rusts.
It has no interest in electricity.
Like rock it has learned to wait.
Like water it takes no pleasure in waiting.
Like me it wants to burn in the old way.

Or "words of love,
soft and tender?"

Some days every message I open
reminds me of Walden Pond or
William Blake or sweet Emily.

Some days this comforts me.

God words,
they say,
are human love.

How safe I feel in this town,
patient and modest as a cow,
all its messages bland as milk.

To wander through so many days
warm, well-fed, and bearing
no visible wounds: incredible.

> God is a human
> love word
> they say

Left alone, I feed myself too much,
rush through my duties and spend hours
in aimless self-indulgence.

Vast rolls of internal commentary unreel
and dissolve into oblivion, some
quite eloquent for work improvised
from such mundane material, so far
from another breathing bleeding soul.

> God is
> a human word
> love says.

III.

CONTEMPLATION WITH DISTANT SCENES AND LOON

All day I've been an old parchment written on
too many times: rain forest outside Ketchikan

glowing like green stars; slopes of the Gaisberg
and the Watzmann looming like a family of ice giants

as we climbed; the hemmed-in ribbon of woods
two blocks from home on Riley Creek. And now

in the shadows of Horseshoe Lake, the silent trees
lie out on the water like dancers. Lily pads

and watergrass rest and waver on the surface.
They register everything, remember nothing,

make what they need from what they are given.
I'll sleep poorly in my borrowed tent,

dream of some western mountain I've seen
only from an airplane. The old trees

and older stones will offer themselves to anyone
willing to pull an oar over and over against

the slate-gray water. Above me the murmur of others,
the clink of pots. Soon I will climb the bank

and we'll sit and eat together. A loon swims
right up as though in appraisal or approval,

sharp head reflected like a ghost soul in the lake.

Contemplation with Rainy Birdsong

I.
When it stops raining, the loons will barely notice.
When it stops raining I'll push down my hood.

When the rain stops maybe I'll remember
that the fight in the heart is not to complain

unless it's really someone's fault, to notice
the line made by water dripping from the rope

that holds up the tarp that keeps us sort of dry.

2.
The rain will stop and we'll wish it would rain.
It will rain again when we don't want rain

and I'll walk with my sweetie and just as I am
thinking how beautiful she is she will complain

about her hair frizzing everywhere, and I will say
that it foams around her face like an angel's.

3.
When it rains the low camp bird will come out unhappy
to search among the roots and stones,

and the white-throated sparrow whose song
is common as air in these trees will sing it

like it's never been heard before
and will be lost forever when he lets it go.

Contemplation with Borrowed Tent

Where did the birds go when the wind
put their little nest down-side up

in the low blueberries? Had they left already?
I want to think they need no single home,

that when they tire they settle anywhere
and then sail off in their dreamboats

to no place I can name. But my friends
all know I'm often wrong, I think everything

will work out just because I don't want
to fix it myself. I don't even know the time

but I'm weary, I hope to sleep tonight,
my borrowed bag is waiting

in my borrowed tent and I am not
a bird, I want a home however frail,

however temporary. On the far shore
just above the trees is a lens of open sky

like the entrance to paradise,
like the doorway to the dream I had

last night when I didn't even think
I was sleeping. And the fresh wood

I had piled on the fire cracked
at last and broke into flame.

CONTEMPLATION ON RULES AND LINES

One law for lion and ox is oppression, but of which one?

The ghost of William Blake, gnarled and smiling in the hollow between tree and stone, refuses to say.

One law for water and rock is precision. Whenever they meet, water does all the talking.

Another law is rubbing. Another can be spoken clearly only in loon. Another takes 300 Earth years to state in full.

A lost fishline dangles like a strand of the golden thread, left behind by a traveler who went back home with nothing but bug bites and a solid case of jock itch.

I'm not so careful myself but I wish I were, and I tell myself that counts for something.

The wind's law is this: Be yourself, and I will show you what that is.

The water's law is this: Tell me anything. Only my face will answer. I will hold the little ones in their little boats, I will let them go where they choose if they have the strength.

I will tell them what they must know, even if it breaks their backs or their hearts.

I will tell them what they want to know only if they ask very softly, and more than once.

CONTEMPLATION WITH WEARY TRAVELERS

For three days the wind has been everywhere, bringing nothing but rain and confusion.

Bedraggled families and clusters of beefy guys circle their canoes around the lakes, but the sites have all been taken by other bedraggled families and church groups trying in vain to dry their socks and cook their lentils and freeze-dried lasagna.

Even the white-throated sparrow seems resigned to despair and one drop after another falling right on his head.

Hollow out as many trees as you like, scrape the bark from twigs to find something dry enough to catch, hope you have enough fuel for the stove.

Hope the great cloudburst doesn't come while you're on the water.

Hope that when the others wake they'll be smiling and ready to cook.

Remember the burned spot where there might have been a cabin, the fish parts and quarter tomato and onion skins left by the last camper.

Take a compass reading from your last shower to the marshy shore filled with sedge, just where a moose would graze if it was your time to see one.

Contemplation on Rain and Religion

I've decided that I'm religious but not spiritual.
— Gregory Wolfe

I always feel more religious in the sunshine,
especially if it's not hot and the place is pretty

and most people can't afford to get there or just
don't bother. Morning has broken and all that.

And so the rattle of rain on the tarp doesn't really
make me count my blessings, the stray drops

beading my borrowed rain pants don't bring
me bliss, the fact of fewer mosquitoes

than yesterday does not make my heart leap up.
But I know this: one day I must learn

to give up for good on getting dry,
to love the hiss of water falling into water,

the gray lake meeting the gray rain,
so little between them, our slender place

between the great sky and the stones.
Hold tight, I tell my heart, here we go.

CONTEMPLATION ON LAKE INSULA

The dreaming memory of Lake Insula barely contains
our two canoes struggling between its islands

one windy afternoon, stopping for logan bread
and peanut butter in a sheltered bay. The stars

she gathers on clear nights, the moon, the water striders
and whirligigs that touch without expecting more:

these fill her dreams. The trees that the wind
takes down to give her, yes, and many things

she will never show to you or me. The little island
called The Rock, a few tons of soil and firs and sedge

clinging tight, and blueberries so tiny that a hundred
are not a handful — even The Rock is not friend or lover,

just the neighbor she cannot avoid entirely.
She is working very carefully to wear him down.

The wind is on her side. But for now her dream
and her memory are a vast hum, a long slant

of light, green things and others making
what they are not yet from what already is,

what was, what burns hot, what burns not at all,
what sleeps in the wet heart of the world.

IV.

CUYAHOGA EVENING WITH DISTANCE AND ABSENCE

In the rosy dusk the meadows steamed like horses hot from a day's work.
The giant burdock's roots were gulping the day's rain, if what happens

silent and underground can be called gulping. The last light reddened
and fell, and the old coliseum site was clothed in a mist like history released,

like a huge slow sigh. The hunt for the missing woman filled the papers,
but she was nowhere I could see. On Oak Hill Road I thought of hiking

the steep dark trail to Furnace Run, but instead I drove on down the hill
and left on Everett Road to the white house where I've lived twice before,

a few days at a time. It's sweet to be alone in mist, all the terrors hidden.
I called home busy. My wife's trying to keep her parents bucked up,

properly medicated, and out of assisted living, all from far away.
So I sat on the porch with the agreeable frogs, counted cars turning right

onto Riverview Road. If all the world were just this way, there'd be
too much traffic but plenty of rain, frogs and giant burdock. The phone

was still busy. The dead woman had been dumped a mile from me,
but nobody knew yet. Some loud insect scouted the porch. No traffic,

no frogs for a moment. The dust was mostly settled, the ball games all over.
Mist spun around the yard lights, a filmy bridgework into the night.

SOMETHING THE WINTER WREN DIDN'T SAY

Any place to sit will do because I aim to disobey,
to disappear, to wait and listen till the hard earth

shudders open like a touch-me-not. Rocks
like spilled treasure waiting for the dragon,

like junker cars rolled downhill toward the crusher,
like science waiting for fiction. Whose idea was it

anyway, to wait so long, to let all this accumulate?
The tanager and the winter wren both want to sleep,

but neither is willing to give up the last word.
I'm more like the rocks — I've slept for centuries.

But I remember now: after a hundred good nights
our lover the moon got bored and nudged

this corner down, roughed things up to mark
her place just in case, and went away.

She hasn't come close to us since. We made
many low songs almost as sweet as the wren's

and the tanager's, desperate to lure her back,
but we see her roaming through the wild sky

and know she's seeing that bully sun,
letting him drive his hot car a million miles an hour

with no seat belt, parking in a black hole
and spreading wide for him, riding him till

she glows so white and wet the world cracks and bellows,
and the rain pours down to turn our rage to tears.

EVENING WITH LONG BOOKS

Each man is a half-open door
leading to a room for everyone.
　　　　— *Tomas Tranströmer*

My friends say Tolstoy really got into the heads
of his female characters. They give him credit.
They talk dreamily of the books they love,

books so long only two will make a whole course.
This seems to me like making twelve gallons of chili
and eating nothing else till it's gone, but I smile

and listen. My friends are smarter than me
and more patient, surely. I'm the only guy
in the house tonight so I get my own room

with a good foam mattress, a bad desk, windows
that open on other rooms. I make up the bed
and lie down with Tranströmer's poems,

ten or twenty lines on a page, fewer words
in fifty years than Tolstoy or George Eliot put down
in a decent work week. *Each man is a half-open door.*

The door to my room is cracked open,
lights blaze outside. My friends are all upstairs.
If I don't shut the light off, no one will.

The wind will settle toward morning, the waves
begin again to spell their single complicated word.
Waiting for the ferry we watched a hawk

try to lift a four-foot snake from the shallows,
drop it, circle, swoop and grab again and lose
its grip and veer away. Oh, how sweet would

that meat have been, how grand a feast, how we
would have cracked and sucked the bones,
how long we could have made that story last.

Island Morning with Occasional Metaphor

The stones throw their shadows abruptly
Like objects on the surface of the moon.
— Tomas Tranströmer, Outskirts

All this time treating the world like a book whose tedious plot
involves years of bleary routine and brief whirls of overstimulation

and terror. Then last night the door between sleep and conversation
an inch ajar for hours, and now three tiny silent birds who leave

the branches rocking when they fly, and the sweatshirt
I don't need, and the duck's wing tips stirring it ahead,

and my hands trying to do the same. The private road I don't take
but imagine how if confronted I'd say *Is this place for sale?*

The jogger whose Ipod is flying mother nature's silver seed
to a new home. The bird house in the bird preserve — empty,

weathered, necessary — before I enter the cool woods
where the path dwindles to nothing, and walk a long way

sometimes on deer trails sometimes not, clutching a twig
that broke off in my hand, and find the shingle beach at last

where great drifts down the beach are not sand but shells
bleached pale as new snow, crisp and dry as a year's worth

of poems almost good enough to keep. And a hundred
cormorants swirl, turn, settle in the iron-gray water,

where whole cities and forests of cloud range off above
the lake, and four dark boats move like people in a novel

I found entrancing but had to put back on the table when
someone called out hurry, we'll be late, get in the car.

KELLEY'S ISLAND ELEGY WITH WIND AND INNUENDO

Never mind the angels — no one will hear. I won't hear
myself. This deafening dirty roar was the wind's idea,

but the water agrees over and over, then says *wait*
when it's far too late, the sand already all up in its skirts.

The trees nod but they're troubled, they almost
remember the last time this happened. The gulls

skate sideways, sure that something interesting
will turn up. For once the breakwater is earning its keep.

And yet a hundred yards inland it's all hearsay and
innuendo, rumors the low weeds toss off without

a thought. One more scandal, one more line buzzing
in a starlet who forgot her panties on purpose, what's

it to them? At the boardwalk's end a soggy trail,
and a sudden white tail. A flight of cormorants surfs

the torrent south, hoping this is as lucky as it seems.
On the alvar shore it's hard not to believe the waves

are pouring down a long slow hill, they bruise
and bounce so full of sand, so angry, so off-kilter,

in such a hurry and then so lost about their next move.

LISTENING FOR ORPHEUS

O you lost God! You neverending trace!
Only because hatred tore and scattered you
are we hearers now and a mouth for nature.
— Rilke, Sonnets to Orpheus 26

This room with unplayable piano and diabolical fold-out sofa,
this room with awful wallpaper and fine ornate molding.

Room in the middle of an island quiet as underground,
quiet as space in the last hour before sleep.

Room full of vanished strays and sleepers, absent outsiders,
sad aunts and gay uncles, traces in the corners, skin-flecks

under the table, under the sofa of ghosts who slipped away
intact and happy enough to have escaped the maenads,

to have been neither torn nor scattered, neither lost
nor divine. To elude the furies should be blessing enough.

To sleep in a room where even the sound of the rain
reaches only your dreams. To dream a dark street

shining beneath the old and erotic trees, to dream
a music born of wood and air, fire and muscle, leaping

and astonished, three voices none of them your own.

OH

And you say Oh, then Oh!
        — *Keith Ratzlaff, Ending in Oh*

Rocks like Jeffers described: hard headed, stiff witted,
but not chatterers or fools. Not easy to walk on them,

but not dull either. East, the mainland is lost in murk
and haze. West, the last sun tints a few tentative clouds.

Yesterday I read Robert Hass's account of the difference
between "Oh" and "O," which was offered with complete

confidence and matched my own views not at all.
The heat is supposed to break tomorrow. A family

of otters prowls just offshore, diving for dinner, staying close.
The low thrum of the freighters never quite stops.

How many steps between vast calm and total panic?
When I say "Oh" I mean "O," if Bob Hass is around.

If Ratzlaff is around, I don't know what I mean.
I couldn't hear the freighters at first, and now

I can't stop listening. This long rock, like an enormous
baguette gone stale. Like a fossil finger pointed

toward Bellingham or Blaine or Mt. Baker. Like
the colored pencil God threw down when it was time

to quit on the shore line and make some seals and gulls
and crabs. And now the cloud bank over White Rock

has burst into color — another few miles is nothing for the sun —
and the little people-lights hug the skin of the world

like God knows what, like fireflies or deer eyes
on the road, like embers of a fire left to burn out

on a windy afternoon, no rain for weeks, the forest
so dry, oh, the arbutus leaves rustling, Oh, O.

INTERIOR ARCHEOLOGY

There's the old photograph of the CPS camp in the mountains,
the barracks snow-frosted, pines clutching the slope. The men

must be inside around the stove arguing about Caesar
and Jesus, or out splitting wood, or escaped on the daily freight

that hauls coal through the eastern desert to the smoky cities.
The men carry *We will not kill* like the mark of some

un-American beast, marking them as weak and strong at once.
Now I own so many books that they keep falling off the table,

right in the middle of the distant, inexcusable news.
I have hardened my heart only a little, said that bastard Jeffers.

What happened to the life I lived in the forest, when I knew
how to make snares and where to find the salt lick?

We walked together then, happy or not. When we killed
something big, everybody feasted, told stories, then

made love all night. When we lost someone we closed up
the circle and kept going. How did we forget so much?

THE PASSENGER

I.

He sat for an hour in the back seat — cramped, but warm,
and the rain was someone else's problem. When the car stopped,

he stepped out into the darkness, followed his companion
through the automatic doors. Inside, there was light

and several lines, then another seat. Then he was driven
again, and washed up gently against his destination.

2.

The world is charged with so much ... where do the physical
and the metaphysical cross? He thinks he used to know.

But the blind and suicidal Gloucester was sure he'd reached
the cliff-edge, so vivid was Edgar's description:

*The crows and choughs that wing the midway air
Show scarce so gross as beetles* ... This room seems steady,

but so did the jet plane, its roaring constant as any waterfall.
Wordsworth knew that the memory of landscape

is far stronger and stranger than the scene itself —
the hidden valley, a few sheep, kites, the heap

of undressed stones. No tender tendril of vine
can erase the sense of loss, abridge the brutalities

of late capitalism, or run the coal companies out of Kentucky.
How does history alter the interior life? The suffering

of thousands makes a bed of nails, said Gide,
one can almost sleep upon it, but one man's sorrow,

one woman's, is a spike through the heart.

3.
The passenger forgot his toothbrush and has twice
brushed with his index finger, not too well.

He could find another but walked across the street instead.
The poetry of earth is never dead, said Keats,

as if the poetry had been there all the time, as if language
is of the earth, like sunflowers and crickets and the dust of stars.

4.
Learning two words for every thing makes one
less sure of anything, and more tender. A new language

opens another world, if we learn to trust it.
I dropped the pen. The pen, it fell from me.

The yellow of summer is not the yellow of winter.
The terror of these suburban zones,

without a weed or a sidewalk: where will
we walk, when we can't bear to look?

5.
The passenger scrawls uneasily with a person
in the chair on each side, stranded as they all are

in their waking lives. When the word *bone* is spoken,
he tries to figure the weight and density of bones

in the room, to calculate the pounds of flesh,
the pairs of jeans and shoes, the memories

and genitals and sweet tendrils of hair escaping
from pins and clips. The passenger lapses again

into dumb Whitmanian tenderness. Nobody notices.

6.
A thing is an announcement, someone announces.
Try to live in the uninterpreted world, said Rilke *auf Deutsch*.

Warranted when used well, said the sticker within the clock.
The passenger is taking bad notes. *When the din of thinking*

dies back, one can begin to listen. I came to you Lord
because of the fucking reticence of the world.

It is music that opens the doorway.
The hide of the deer shivered. The bright eye was still.

7.
He fears he has entered irrevocably the world
of the gray scale, where the spirit finds no firm ground,

where the angels have no names. He may never leave
the vast middle room with its bright lights

and no windows, its many chairs facing all
in the same direction. When the lights go out

they are blinded for a moment, but then everything
swims back, little changed. The passenger is not lost,

nor found. He is the Fool, the card without a number.
No, of course he isn't. He is a question

without a question mark. He is nodding, or trying
to rub away a headache. *You think you have no map,*

but your life is the map, says the voice from
the front of the room, whose face is a mask

with bees and splinters of glass behind.

8.
The truck last night went by, dragging a chain.
The wick curled cold in the kerosene lamp.

The passenger took the gum his friend offered,
then had to hold it in his mouth for what

seemed like hours. Often in his other life
he finds himself standing in the front of the room.

Gum and *Gun* are closer in English than in
the other world. The first woman scribe

took the mikveh, the purifying bath,
then spent a whole day writing nothing

but the name of God. The passenger bathes daily,
and feels refreshed but not purified.

He is an Anabaptist. He was sprinkled
long ago, and told that once was enough.

He wears a shirt that says *Beauty will save the world*
beneath his other shirt, where no one will see.

9.
And now everyone will leave the room. And now
his other life will resume. And now the music will begin,

like a doorway or a pattern drawn in colored sand,
like wind heeling a small boat close to disaster,

driving it into the open sea. The passenger
will listen, the salty spray on his lips.

Notes from the Faculty Meeting

After eight years of bounty, the cow has dried up.

Behind the great man the shield icon pulsed, patient as a heart.

Like seeds, some ideas appear whole and undamaged
but will never sprout.

Any form of motion draws the eye.

So far, every page of this yellow pad has torn ragged.

This troubles me more than it should.

I vowed to hold my breath until I heard a concrete noun.

Does "things" count? "Students?" "Projections?"

My attempt at narrative, jumbled already, was interrupted
by the need to applaud.

The phrase "difficult challenge" was not followed
by showers of gold.

"Forming a task force" did not lead to "pursue the Great One."

Most students believe they're more honest than most students.

After a national search, we hired Randy's brother.

MARCH ODE

Free beer tomorrow, and no more rain than the creek can carry off.
Daffodils will swell and break loose. The maple seeds, soggy

in the muck, will remember why they left home, smile shyly
and spread wide. Free beer tomorrow. Whoever left the coffee cup

by the drinking fountain will remember and come back.
The whispering planet will shudder and relax a little. No one

will expect me to offer counsel on paragraph coherence or standards
for tenure. I will remember where I buried my soul, in the woods

along the creek, and when I peel away the duct tape it will be
only a little rumpled, a little miffed. Free beer tomorrow,

and at Luke's the townies and college kids will exchange free pitchers
and toast their luck. Luke himself will walk between the tables,

passing out baskets of popcorn and peanuts. The storms will leave
the fields moist but not muddy. The tractors will run forever

on a single tank of diesel, the milkweed, buttonweed, and bindweed
cling to the fencerows of their own sweet will. Pheasants and foxes

will cavort and chortle, and monarchs proclaim the acceptable era
of orange-winged lords. Free beer tomorrow, and whoever left us

so long ago will remember at last, and turn and start back. I will ask
and it will be given, and the shouts and murmurs of the happy drinkers

will wash hin and yon until we are only the cups to be filled,
only the flutes that quiver to the skillful breath, becoming song.

INTIMATIONS OF ETERNITY
FROM THE SUBURBAN BALCONY

How to imagine the undefended life in the snarl of the city?
We must close all the windows at night, they say, or
the dark men will come right in. That voice this morning,

I almost cried, *David!* He's long dead; it was just some stranger.
Once I glimpsed eternity in the drizzle that sifted through
the soft leaves of Bear Creek Park. Then years went by

without a sound. Still I trust that on some ordinary day
the gates will splinter, and faith will be something we can
toss away, a child's blanket worn down to a few threads.

Even now the green & white taxi might be bearing
the True One down 108 Avenue toward the shrieking children.
The ice cream truck could give up that awful song and launch

into the lost cadence. We could shake our heads right after lunch,
realize how easy it would be to give up pain for beauty.
The child who's too big for training wheels might just laugh,

stop his little bike on the sidewalk and fix everything at once.

No Boundaries

This is only an outline of the great scheme,
made even harder by the gentle eyes that cross

mine on every corner. I stumble, recover,
but they dissolve into the press of strangers,

familiar colors, tremors and aftershocks
still troubling the streets, tumbles of fruit

and books, sharp smell of broken concrete.
The light enlarges everything except cooking pots

and the supplies of rice. Even the hardest benches
are full, thin thighs pressed together in the heat.

We are not far from water, but we are thirsty.
We are blessed by the sun, but not filled.

A young woman in red threads her way
toward me — I could almost speak to her —

then the crowd shifts and she disappears.
Not even a Bible can cure a stone. My mouth

gives nothing away. Words fill me like citrus,
but my lips have closed. My tongue remembers

the rush of water, the taste of powder
and dust, the bitter instruction of the guns.

Slippery Intimations on the Flood Plain

We moved into the soft evening
along the little path beside the creek
then into the grass

It seemed I was just learning to walk
to fall constantly and catch myself every time
I kept going
always too fast or too slow

There was a woman with two dogs
Kecia's friend hollered at her
The stones were cold and solid and welcome
A little wind

I'll write blind, as I've done all day
I am learning to keep going
but not to be patient

My kids used to play in these scruffy woods
among the trash and flinders of one flood after another

Flood plain trees are conservatives of the old sort
they tolerate bats and getting their feet wet now and then
hate chainsaws and garlic mustard

My neck is tense again but I'm all in
a pair in the hole
This hand might settle everything

A million breaths taken and released into the slippery night
Ink drawn out of the darkness
onto the bare page

On the flood plain
whispers of eternity edge in
ten of us breathing together
barely warming the rough stones

The lamps and tables of the great world
dusted and trimmed and set for company

On the River of Doubt with TR and the Boys

We were still wholly unable to tell where we were going or what lay
ahead of us. Round the camp-fire, after supper, we held endless dis-
cussions and hazarded all kinds of guesses on both subjects. ... We
had entered a land of unknown possibilities.
   — *Theodore Roosevelt,*
    "Through the Brazilian Wilderness," 1919

Our plan: to follow down-stream an unknown river, broken
by cataracts and rapids, rushing through mountains
whose existence has never been even guessed.

Not long after we left town, we passed a single hillock.
Then, vast stretches of marshy forest.

Our boots were sturdy and our rifles waterproof.

I killed a wood-ibis on the wing with the handy little Springfield,
then lost all credit by a series of inexcusable misses.

Brilliantly colored parakeets and trogons,
and the slow current quickened.

My books included the last two volumes of Gibbon,
the plays of Sophocles, More's "Utopia," Marcus Aurelius,
and Epictetus, the two latter lent me by a friend.

I will not even mention our difficulties
with the natives, or Douglas, who persisted
in assailing the cook concerning his biscuits.

But I see that I *have* mentioned poor Douglas.

The boroshudas left marks that lasted for weeks;
I did my writing in headnet and gauntlets.

The deep, sheer-sided, narrow channel.

The arduous hauling of the dugout canoes
through woods and over rocks.

Days of delay when the worst boat split entirely
and another must be fashioned from scratch.

In most respects our party meshed wonderfully;
we suffered only one death by drowning and one homicide.

Poor Simplicio, his life beaten out on the boulders.
One mourns, but mourning cannot interfere with labor.

The unhappy murderer begged to surrender,
but to take him aboard would have endangered us all.

It was very lovely on the river when the sun
had burned up the fog, and looked through it
in a red splendor. The great trees, the network
of bush ropes, the caverns of greenery.

In the end we abandoned all inessential gear,
yet the rapids proved impossible to run.

To lose one's outfit and provisions — disaster.
To go too slowly, exhaust the provisions,
go forward weakened — the same.

Olive and copper and ebony, the men's skins
glistened as if oiled, and rippled
with the ceaseless play of the thews beneath.

The ragged bugler kept his bugle to the very end.

The great naked flats of sandstone …

The stretches of fine sand, the coarse grass over them . . .

And when finally we emerged, we carried something
new — ourselves, perhaps. We knew the River of Doubt
as we had found it. I dream still of our tents

and shoes mouldering near a termite mound,
the broken canoe already going back to pulp,
shell casings splitting the light at sundown.

EVENING RHAPSODY BETWEEN
MADISON AND WHITEWATER

Too much of anything is better than Milwaukee's Best
when the first snow hits in November and I'm already sick

of winter, when it's stone dark by five, when the country roads
are lettered and empty and I should have obeyed the instructions,

should have turned around, should have done it all right,
every road swerves and twists and with each little town

I have to stop and squint at the atlas, astonished when somehow
I find them all on the map, somehow each turn brings me closer

to the pretty clerk in the low-cut blouse who will hand me
the key card with a smile like the deluxe continental breakfast,

somehow not a single deer pops sudden and solid into my headlights,
and the aching ball joint holds through each and every curve,

and there's room in the ditches for a lot more empties — not that
I'm drinking — and I keep glimpsing water along the road,

glints and shivers of light and the roads curving among them
as I sweep through darkness, and I am never truly lost,

not after the late moon rises in the east like God's thumbnail,
like a medallion of embossed paper torn carefully in half.

V.

MOONS

Music, states of happiness, mythology, faces worn by time, certain
twilights and certain places, all want to tell us something …
  — Borges, "The Wall and the Books"

— *for Bill Keeney*

Until this moment all of this had never been — road noise,
dusky machinery hemming the quarry, grain that falls and rises
and falls again as the harvest spills into the proper chambers.

And the shutdown factory, and the electric plant torn down
years ago, and some of the bastards newly and partly displaced
from power, and my glasses fogged and the quarry dark and chill

and ready for anything except fight or flight. And now what?
and now? This fall a heron found every backyard pond in town
and cleaned them out in a week, vexing and conflicting

my nature-loving friends. It could be another sign of the next wave,
along with the yard sign I planted for the first time I can remember
for a guy who won. *Don't change the weatherman,* said our wise

and expensive visitor, *change the wind. You have to understand,*
said the somber man, *We need our secrets.* These days I come out
of my office at dusk and walk home kicking leaves in the golden

half-light, wishing it would linger. It doesn't. I circle the quarry
and remember how I'd meet Bill, patiently shuffling one way as I went
the other. He was in Colombia the first time his heart kicked back

and we thought he was finished. He came back thinner and quit running,
but made ten more years, showed up everywhere around town
with his spunky and irreverent wife. Early Sunday we heard

the sirens, and at prayer time the pastor stood in his dark suit,
breathing too hard, and told us all. We paused and then went on.
A cottontail startles up, bobbles ahead of me, veers away through a gap

in the fence. Not long ago, after careful investigation, we learned
that the earth has no smaller moons, and the moon has no moons at all.

ADDITIONAL ASSERTIONS ON SOUL

Only moving does it have a soul.
— Pablo Neruda, "Ode to Bicycles"

1) All stones, even those from the moon, must share a single soul.

2) Dragonflies each have the soul of another, and spend their lives chasing their own.

3) Barns have souls until the main timber breaks.

4) Birds have souls only when singing, flying, or at rest.

5) Butterflies are so light because they abandon their souls at birth.

6) Automobiles have souls made of grease and fire, just like us.

7) The heron's soul is all bone and feathers, an excellent mother despite its lack of hands and breasts.

8) The tiger lily's flower is tender and sweet on the tongue, and its soul likewise.

9) We believe the earth has a soul, but nobody has ever gotten its attention.

10) The many tiny souls of the grass were at perfect ease until Whitman began to ask questions.

11) The air is one wild soul looking blindly for the lost one.

12) And the water, oh it carries many souls, but keeps none for itself.

KANSAS STREET, NORTH NEWTON, NOVEMBER 26

Things seem a little plainer here: the low grass
a uniform brown, leaves gone from the cottonwoods.

But there's the cypress still holding its reddish needles,
and snow in shady patches like threadbare blankets,

and the woman in a pink coat walking, and two crows
flapping and calling overhead, and the twin locomotives

crossing the trestle, hauling only each other
and their paired whistle, and minor birdsongs

in the quiet afterwards. And jumbled driftwood
where the trestle stopped it, and creek water

slipping quietly between. *I don't much like
airplanes any more,* N. told me this morning.

I don't either, but I like arriving elsewhere,
a place with sky and high clouds, tracery

of limb and branch against them, the doppler
of a small plane and the hunch of the earphoned biker,

hood pulled tight, pumping toward Newton.
It's all plain and simple, every unrepeatable

tapestry of bark and sunlight, air and deep cool earth,

the odds against any of this a zillion to one,

and the pair of crows perched so high they let me
walk right under them, and the quick sparrows

finding so many places to rest, so many reasons to fly.

Story Problem near Vancouver Island

After enough years even the clearcuts
are beautiful, at least in the hazy distance.
Consider this: If a man walks

seven times around the top deck
while the ship travels southwest at
fourteen knots, and six times around

make a mile, and the ocean
is placid as the Buddha's soul,
and the islands slip past like

long-haired girls on the evening beach,
how long must he walk before
the true admonition dances

through the noisy silence?
One island may hide another island.
One mountain may hide another mountain.

How long the world has swayed,
how lightly it rolls and swings
and bears us up, all mixed

and shifting, separate and one.
There is only one ocean,
and it hides itself almost perfectly.

In the south a vast cloud moved
above the long ridge, a ship driving
through waves of cliff and rock,

bearing east with its cargo
of faint hopes and raw soapstone
and ivory only the faithful

may touch without breaking.

On the Way to the Glacier

I.

The ocean said: it's simple, but will take years to explain.
The mountain said: never mind, you'll never get it anyway.

We took the train despite the old ones' warnings, creaked up
the coast range and rolled through the high, soggy valley

where the leaning peaks wore their fog caps all day long.
The fjord wind kept changing its view of all the tough issues,

the brilliant sun explained everything in one long sentence,
and we didn't nod off even in the drowsy afternoon.

When we left the train we forgot it all at once, and the clouds
rolled over like the capes the on-board magicians use

when they're not demanding applause or displaying their torsos,
and the thin streak of light that leaked in from the north said,

Stay awake, don't falter, be ready to take to the boats.

II.

So I faced back like the Angel of History while you read
and the old ones rested. We knew we must cherish them

even when they forgot the directions, complained of obscure pains
and refused to get off the ship. We saw them to bed and walked

on the wild top deck where the sun loitered until 10:30.
The horizon was a perfect seam for the eye to follow,

searching for the manic portal. The ship never faltered
and the world opened easily and slid shut behind us,

over and over. I drank coffee on the fantail and scowled at anyone
who approached, the staff did not try to comfort me, the breeze

took my cup when it was empty, the wreckage of our passage
spilled out behind, all foam and desolation too deep to reckon.

And somewhere forward the old ones dreamed of their courtship,
how he sang "Goodnight Irene" for her in Yarrow, and then

woke to wonder when they'd promised to meet us for dinner.

III.

And down one deck the wind was only a rumor and the banks
rushed by on all sides, steep as a hasty marriage, and on the ridge line

trees pointed like spears or signals or the last row of the crowd.
We came in fast and left the same way, touched almost nothing,

washed our hands often with soap and water. We ordered
everything on the menu and our waiter pleased the children

with his napkin tricks, the shoe, the mouse, the rose. It's good
to serve, and to make a thing into another. His children study

in Manila with the money he sends back. He was below decks,
off duty, when we stopped to watch the glacier calve,

its music slow and deep as any great fall. *I remember,*
said the guide who came onboard to explain this to us,

when I was young, I slept on the island in the seal camp,
and all night each night the white thunder filled our sleep.

PASSAGE

On the swift cruise there was only time and water, twin mothers
of an anxious son. And money. In the long end of day we pushed

right at the sun and failed again except at witness, the beauty
softened by mist and latitude until we could almost bear it. What else

could we do? We could drain the tanks in a long stern chase
and never get closer, two-footed, chilled, awkward as we are,

the vast ship tiny on the sea. When the captain spoke we couldn't
understand. When the cruise director spoke we didn't listen.

There was free champagne but we didn't get any. If there were stars,
we missed them. On the sea only the surface matters anyway,

the whitecaps a fresh sign of the spirit, happy in the cold surge,
foaming toward the full north, sliding calm as paradise away

as we watched for a tail, a spout, some sign from underneath.
So the wake curled endlessly, the radars whirled, meals were

heaped and spread all day, and the servants pretended to love the work.
The fog had its charms and the chill breeze too, and we learned

that the coast range and the island range allow anyone passage.
They were parents aging gently, good providers with little to say.

Then they were long books written in the old tongue, the one
God made up before she had company. Then they were houses

for any spirit brave enough to make the journey. Then the fog
was laughter, was music, was long hair combed out damp at the fire.

And we walked the slick deck in the long dusk, and the ship
bore us north, and in the dawn the mountains were tattered sails

at the fringes of memory, and the summer home God built
when all our speaking was too much, and the tousled hair

of a quiet daughter, her face too sweet to bear except in fog.

Afternoon Walk with Mosquitos and Commentary via Simone Weil and Mike Edmiston

The flood left a skim-coat of muck on leaves and branches,
windrows of sticks and drift here and there, and newly hatched

mosquitos in scary abundance — I tried to sit in the woods
by the creek but had a cloud around me whining and nipping

before I even got settled. *The beauty of the world is the mouth*
of a labyrinth. … And there God is waiting to eat you, Simone proclaimed,

so I walked some more, chased a squirrel from two logs drifted
across the lower path. Only two or three mosquitos at a time there.

Very few all summer, the creek bone-dry for weeks, then downpours
all night and brown water roaring all around by morning. *If we can*

build up the levee, stock up on sandbags, and put a shut-off valve
on the sewer, Mike said just this morning, *we can keep the building dry*

next time. I wandered on along the creek — it's down to a trickle again —
and crossed the bridge that was under water two weeks ago.

The day was lovely, sunny, green. I wished for a stiff breeze, or a smudge
pot, or a hide of thick leather. *The great trouble in life,* Simone whispered,

is that looking and eating are two different operations. Nettles flowered
in the beds by the art building. *With a long handle, we can close that valve*

no matter how high the water gets, Mike said. *There are people who try to raise*
their souls like a man continually taking standing jumps, Simone muttered,

in the hopes that he will go right up to the sky. Where was the white butterfly
going, low and straight along the sidewalk? All week the monarchs

had been fluttering in the trees. All summer the turkey vultures have
been soaring past my top-floor window, roosting on the high lantern.

It was a glorious day, if only I didn't mind the insects, if only
I could look and not be eaten. It was impossible not to mind.

DRIFTWOOD

Little slab tossed for a year or ten
in the blue sea, rippled grain and cracks

from drying in the sand —
you could float, almost, on air.

Hollow, with splinters of light inside.
A ship on the inner ocean, a prison

with many doors and few bars,
a bed and a bad meal for any weary soul.

A contour map of oblivion or paradise,
a 3D guide to the holy life,

a single-paged book so dense
it can only be translated into braille or angel.

Suppose the secret is here but if not read tonight
it will be lost forever. Suppose you passed me

on the rocky shore but didn't stop to talk.
Suppose the doorway will not open

without a kiss from the prince's lips
or my common thumb rubbing. Suppose

the oily sheen appears and the stars all
break from their spheres,

whirl and wheel along the rubbled beach,
fire every rock and bleached log,

stain every scrap of driftglass,
etch a red-gold web on every empty walker.

WALK WITH GRAND-DOG AND WALLACE STEVENS

He never supposed divine
Things might not look divine, nor that if nothing
Was divine then all things were, the world itself,
And that if nothing was the truth, then all
Things were the truth, the world itself was the truth.
   — Wallace Stevens

Sea gull quartering the wind. Heron along the shore,
then pinwheeling back, low to the water. Wind in poplar,

cedar, beech, and pine, each speaking in a different voice.
Wind in me, in the book of vanished Stevens, in you —

more voices. Why sort them into human and other?
Even the branches the neighbor brought in his barrow

and piled in a heap while Loki barked at him — even
the cut branches have a voice, though a dry and thin one.

Oh, Stevens, you considered but threw away the idea
that the world itself is the truth. It might have saved you

some trouble. The blue jay and downy woodpecker,
clouds that sift the sunlight into something else,

the ant that tracks the sand and beach grass, six crows
in a dead tree like notes for an unfinished symphony —

all voices that seem true to me. When Loki and I walked
the ravine he roamed ahead, aquiver with attention,

probing for traces and invisible signs. He ranged away
until I called out, turned back only when I yelled, *Loki,*

Loki! looked and loped off to sniff another mystery
involving dirt and leaves and a creature long gone.

I could only watch and call, having no leash, no hold
on him except my little voice and his willingness to listen.

All I saw really was Loki's seeing, snuffling through
birches and hemlocks, over the old earth for remnants

made as others walked, sniffed, pissed, as the buried
water bubbled up, filled the pools, trickled on its way.

MEDITATION IN GLEN PARK
WITH SPRINGS AND BAD NEWS

> *We are in and of the world, materially embedded in the same rain-*
> *drenched field that the rocks and the ravens inhabit … . All our*
> *knowledge, in this sense, is carnal knowledge.*
> — David Abram, *Becoming Animal*

Season of white butterflies, common, light and lovely.
Of beech trees split at the ground so that they might

almost be men, almost be women. I ran here, then walked,
then finally sat still. Trickle of water, whisper of wind,

creak of distant bird, slope full of hemlocks — not
soldiers but protectors, not heroes but guardians.

When we sat at the springs Karen said, *This is a thin spot*
and I knew what she meant but asked her to explain.

I tried to talk about my summer reading, that I had learned
again that the world is alive, all of it, and full of sense,

but the words rang so thin and feeble that I stopped,
and we sat in the green shade and worried uselessly

about her new bad news. And the cold water rose
through sand, blinked in the beads of sun that sifted

through leaves, went quiet, obedient and perfect
on its way. Once every story had its place, Abram says,

place was mnemonic to the story. I can say only bits
and pieces from this place, high clouds, black squirrel,

ovenbird, dark sand wet across the valley's crease,
clear trickle easing toward the lake. I moved within it all,

neither welcome nor foreign except as I chose, an animal
among the animals, a creature neither great nor small.

In a clearing where a great tree had broken four others,
I thought suddenly that Wallace Stevens asked the right

questions but got the answers wrong. The new bridge
gleamed with its raw lumber, and the idea of a necessary

fiction seemed absurd. I sat down where the water
was loudest and admired the rough bench, the old dark tiles

that hold the springs until they overflow. These seemed
the necessary constructions, even if no one was there

but me and the butterflies. *I want you to write this place,*
Karen said, *I want to see it in a poem.* Yesterday the doctors

poked G. for the biopsy, tomorrow it's the Cleveland Clinic.
She will not sleep well. Death is not the mother of beauty.

It is its dusty mirror, the crease in the ravine where
the water must run. The white butterfly found a flower,

folded its wings to drink. I bent to the spring, dipped
my hands, cooled my face and sipped and walked away.

Yellow Trail at Laurelville on Rapture Day

I could sit down on this rock, partway up the hill. No time
for the overlook, much less Split Rock. A good day
for caterpillars and new greenery, mushrooms and

puddles just starting to shrink. All this rain, yet one day
we will pray for more. Some say the Rapture is hours away,
but there's no sign yet. It would be some kind of change.

I'm expecting something besides bodies sailing up into
the void, something more like the way new shoots
of mayapple and poison ivy appear out of the muck,

or spring warblers call invisibly from 10:00 high.
Sometimes a leafy branch will wave and beckon
through a window in the trees, then go still. Years ago

I walked up this hill at dawn, sweating with the climb
as I did today, and in the meadow at the top I walked up
on a flock of wild turkeys, as if they'd been waiting for me.